DAYS OF GRATITUDE

A Brief History of a Chesapeake Steamboat

And the Town Named After Her

William M. Denny

American Literary Press
Five Star Special Edition
Baltimore, Maryland

Days of *Gratitude*

Library of Congress
Cataloging-in-Publication Data
ISBN-13: 978-1-56167-996-6

Library of Congress Card Catalog Number:
2007907252

Published by

American Literary Press
Five Star Special Edition

8019 Belair Road, Suite 10
Baltimore, Maryland 21236
Manufactured in the United States of America

ACKNOWLEGEMENTS

The author gratefully acknowledges the assistance of numerous residents of the Town of Rock Hall and Kent County, Maryland, who assisted in the preparation of this history of *Gratitude* by providing background information and local folklore. Of special note are the following: Ann Hennessy, local book author and writer of the newspaper column "Rock Hall Rambler," which is published in the *Kent County News*; Emory "Pie" Edwards, lifelong waterman and Rock Hall icon; and Wm. Norris "Hick" Clark, former waterman and noted Rock Hall Realtor who spent many hours searching through century-old land deeds at the Kent County courthouse to trace the property ownership of various areas described in this book.

The original draft text and format of the book were improved significantly by the extremely helpful suggestions of three experienced editors, namely, Marjorie A. Musil, Carol Hoffner Denny, and Mary K. S. Denny.

CONTENTS

LIST OF ILLUSTRATIONS

LIST OF ILLUSTRATIONS
(continued)

LIST OF ILLUSTRATIONS
(continued)

INTRODUCTION

The western section of the town of Rock Hall, Maryland, now ends at the Chesapeake Bay, directly across the water from the city of Baltimore. But for almost ninety years, the western border of Rock Hall ended at a place called Gratitude, a small, unofficial town that took its name from a steamboat that used to dock there. Neither the steamboat nor the town still exists, except in the memories of long-time residents; and within another generation, even those will be gone.

I became interested in the steamboat *Gratitude* and the town named after her shortly after I purchased a home built over a century ago on the road between Rock Hall and Gratitude. Now officially designated as Maryland Route 20 and locally named Rock Hall Avenue, the road in those days was known as "Steamboat Wharf Road" according to an old survey plot of my property. The name so intrigued me that I began to research the history of steamboats on the Chesapeake Bay and, in particular, the steamboat *Gratitude*, which for over twenty-five years docked each day about one-half mile down the road from my house. Everyone who came to or left from Rock Hall by steamboat during the early 1900s passed by my front door; they represented a pageant of America's history as the country transitioned from a candle and kerosene-lamp agricultural society to an industrial assembly line powerhouse at the beginning of the First World War.

Many searches of libraries and the Internet revealed that the definitive history of the steamboat era on the Chesapeake Bay, and especially that of the steamboat *Gratitude*, was told in five out-of-print books. Over a period of two years, I was fortunate to be able to find and purchase a copy of each book, and the story of *Gratitude* told in the following pages is based substantially on what is written in them. I have extracted the information and assembled it in one place, and combined it with additional historical information, so that anyone in the future who hears a reference made to "Gratitude" in Rock Hall will know what happened there and why.

Gratitude was not a large steamer; in fact, she was smaller than some of the luxury yachts now frequently seen cruising the Bay. But when *Gratitude* began service to Rock Hall in 1887, she was one of the newest and most reliable modes of transportation on the Bay, and her arrival was welcomed by the town. When *Gratitude* got underway from Rock Hall for the last time in 1914, the 100-year history of steamboats on the Chesapeake had already peaked and started to decline; in another fifty years, all the steamboats, both workhorses and floating palaces, would be gone forever.

The steamboat *Gratitude* will never again dock in Rock Hall, and the number of people now alive who had grandparents who rode her across the Bay will soon decrease to zero. But even though she will then be unknown, the enormous contribution *Gratitude* made to the town of Rock Hall and the well-being and prosperity of its citizens will never fade away in the mist of the Bay.

This history is dedicated to all those mariners who served aboard *Gratitude* and worked daily to ensure safe passage across the Bay for the people of Rock Hall and Kent County. Her excellent safety record during those twenty-seven years is a testament to the professional dedication and seamanship of her crews.

The Beginning of an Era

The first voyage of a steamboat on the Chesapeake Bay occurred on Sunday, June 13, 1813, when the steamer *Chesapeake* departed from Baltimore, Maryland, and slowly made her way south to the capital city of Annapolis. The second trip ever made by a steamboat on the Bay was one week later when *Chesapeake* steamed from Baltimore and went east across the Bay to Rock Hall. This historic event continued a tradition, established long before the country was founded, of using the latest technology available to connect Rock Hall with the centers of commerce and power.

George Washington and other revolutionary figures traveled through Rock Hall many times because of its strategic location on the eastern shore of the Bay, from which fast packet sailboats would haul passengers, cargo and communications to other ports. The introduction of steamboats was itself revolutionary because the historic dependency on winds and tides was abolished forever. Fixed schedules for departure and arrival meant that people and businesses could accomplish tasks that were previously impossible.

The success of *Chesapeake* demonstrated both to investors and entrepreneurs that taking a chance on this new mode of travel could result in enormous profits. Various individuals and groups of engineers, ship builders and manufacturers competed to introduce improvements to the new technology and establish routes across the Bay. It took a decade before the next truly significant advances were achieved in boilers, engines, and ship configurations. Acceptance by the public of using steamboats followed these improvements.

The industry grew so rapidly that seventy-five years after the first voyage, and exactly midway in the 150-year history of steamboats on the Chesapeake, more than fifty steamers crisscrossed the Bay each day. It was at this peak of the steamboat era that the steamer *Gratitude* arrived to provide service to Rock Hall and Kent County.

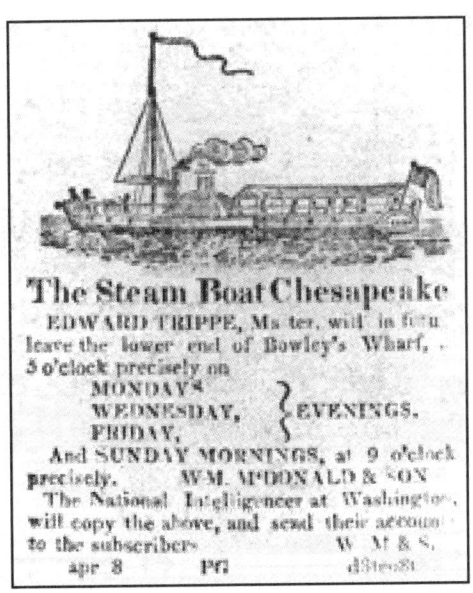

The Steam Boat Chesapeake

EDWARD TRIPPE, Master, will in futu
leave the lower end of Bowley's Wharf, .
5 o'clock precisely on
MONDAYS
WEDNESDAY, } EVENINGS.
FRIDAY,
And SUNDAY MORNINGS, at 9 o'clock
precisely.   WM. M'DONALD & SON
The National Intelligencer at Washingto-,
will copy the above, and send their accoun
to the subscribers   W M & S,
apr 8   PT   d3teo8t

A Model of *Chesapeake* and Advertisement for Rides

7

SS GRATITUDE (1880 – 1926)

The steamer *Gratitude* was built in 1880 in the Kensington section of Philadelphia by shipbuilders Jacob Neafie and Captain John P. Levy, who were among the pioneers of industrial-scale ship production. They built *Gratitude* to provide transportation for passengers and freight on the Delaware River between Philadelphia and Tacony, then a town about seven miles north of the city (and now a part of it). People traveled between Tacony and Philadelphia by boat on the Delaware River because the city government would not allow the Philadelphia and Trenton Railroad (established in 1846) to run trains into the city. Passengers from Trenton, New Jersey, to Philadelphia, Pennsylvania, would travel by train from Trenton to the riverfront in Tacony, then board a steamer that would take them to a wharf at Walnut Street in the center of Philadelphia. Thus, the steamer *Gratitude* was created for a specific service. Even though the trip was a short distance, it was a far superior mode of transportation compared to any other type that was available. The same situation in Kent County, Maryland, was to make *Gratitude* indispensable to Rock Hall for many years.

When *Gratitude* was launched in 1880, she was almost 125 feet long and 21 feet wide at the waterline, displaced 214 tons, and had a single screw propeller (rather than paddle wheels on the side or stern). She had an iron hull, could maneuver in seven feet of water when fully loaded, and cruised at a maximum speed of 13 knots.

Gratitude operated on the Delaware River for only a short time before being sold in 1882 to a company that renamed her *Captain Miller* and used her for travel between New Orleans, Louisiana, and Pensacola, Florida. In 1885, her home port was shifted to Natchez, Mississippi, for a year before she was sold to the Enterprise Transportation Line to operate on the Chester River on Maryland's Eastern Shore.

The first of several serious problems that were to occur in the next four decades happened on April 23, 1887, when *Gratitude* burned while docked at Centreville on the Corsica River (a small river that flows into the Chester River). This first disaster resulted in the steamer starting service to Rock Hall; the next disaster, twenty-seven years later, would result in the steamer ending service to Rock Hall.

After the fire, the owners rebuilt and lengthened the steamer by eight feet, then sold her, on July 2, 1887, to the Centreville and Corsica River Steamboat Company. The new owners renamed her *Gratitude*, and began operating the steamer between Baltimore (Light Street Pier 12), Rock Hall and Centreville. Then, in June 1890, the Chester River Steamboat Company (incorporated January 11, 1867) purchased control of the Centreville and Corsica River Steamboat Company and kept *Gratitude* operating between the same three locations.

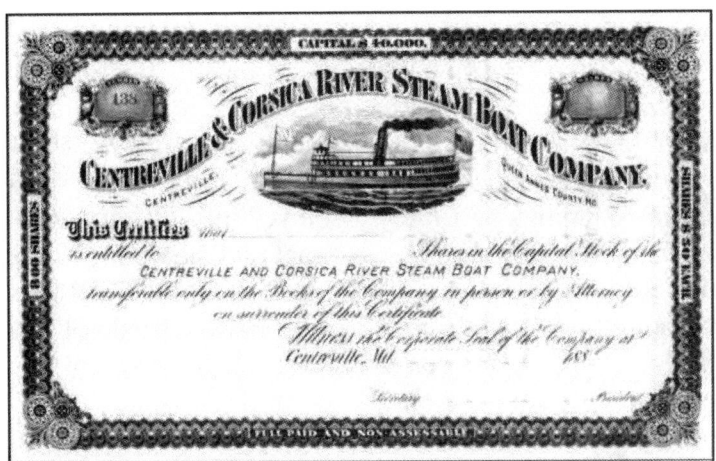

Image of *Gratitude* on a Stock Certificate of the Centreville & Corsica River Steamboat Company

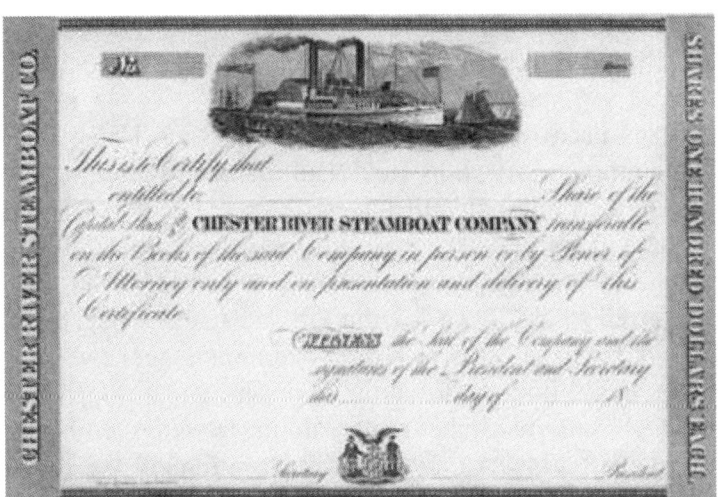

Image of a Side-Wheeler on a Stock Certificate of the Chester River Steamboat Company

Gratitude became the fourth ship to hoist the corporate flag, joining *B.S. Ford* (built 1877), *Corsica* (built 1882), and *Emma A. Ford* (built 1884) flying the red arrow on a white field. All of the four steamers except *Gratitude* had been built by Harlan and Hollingsworth on the Christiana River in Wilmington. *Corsica* enjoyed the distinction of being the only one of the four that did not burn while docked. *B.S. Ford* burned at Chestertown (May 1884) but was rebuilt three years later; *Emma A. Ford* burned at Love Point (March 1909) and was abandoned.

Corsica also had the distinction of being shot at by illegal oyster dredgers who mistook her for a police boat in a fog the night of December 8, 1888. The state of Maryland retaliated two days later by sending an armed, iron-hull tugboat that rammed and sank two of the oyster pirate boats in the Chester River.

The wharf used by *Gratitude* was not in Rock Hall Creek (now commonly known as Rock Hall harbor); rather, it was about one and one-half miles west from the center of town in an area designated by map and chart makers as "Deep Landing" at the entrance to Swan Creek. This location is still referred to as "Deep Landing, Swan Creek, Maryland" (39.1450° N, 76.2600° W) by government agencies that provide daily tide information. Current street maps for Rock Hall designate the road running parallel with the water at that point as Lawton Avenue (although the name of the road was Halsey when *Gratitude* was docking there).

BALTIMORE
MIDDLE RIVER
TUNNEL TOLL
Sparrows Point
Patapsco River
GLEN BURNIE
WASH. EXPWY.
Rock Hall
Church
Centreville
Chester River
Love Point
Queenstown
Stevensville
150
695
151
100
177
2
3
175
18
20
50 301

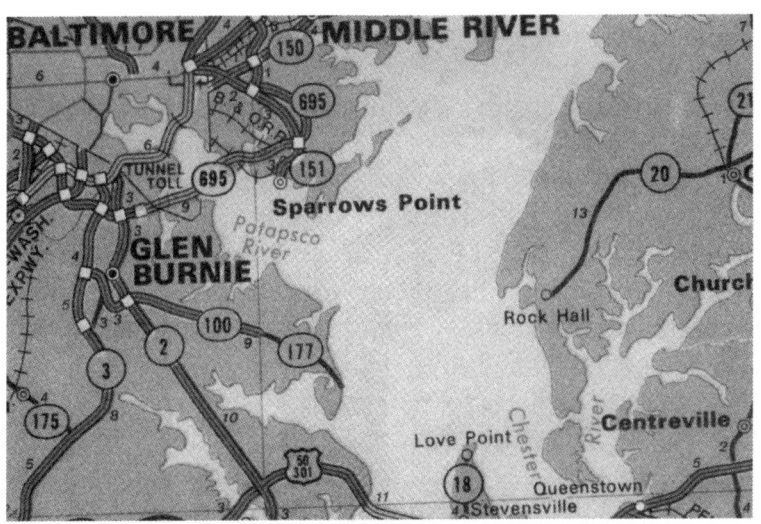

Map Showing Three Ports Served By *Gratitude*: Baltimore, Rock Hall and Centreville

Lawton Ave
New St
Gratitude
20
Wilkins Ave
Beach Rd
Mercer Ave
Bay Rd
Cherry St
Bayside Ave
Walnut St
Haven Rd
N Hawthorne Ave
Boyce Ave
Cottage Ave
Henry Ave
Chester Ave
2nd St
Caroline Ave
E Sharp St

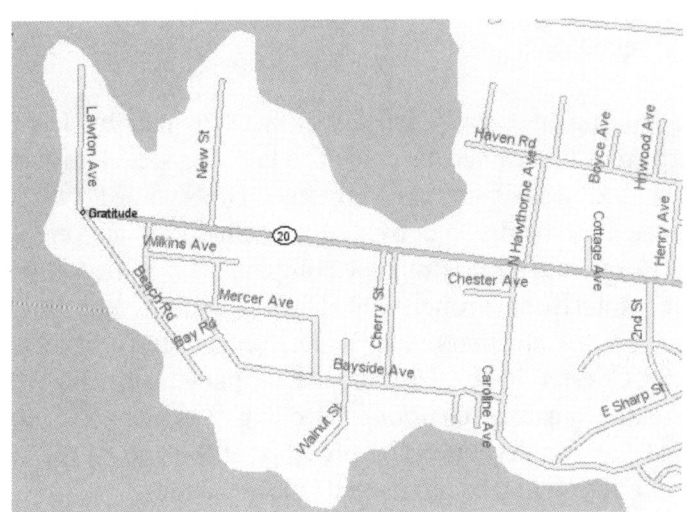

Lawton Avenue in Gratitude (end of MD Route 20)

The reason *Gratitude* docked at Deep Landing was the result of a battle of wills between the first president of the Chester River Steamboat Company, Colonel Budd Sterling ("B. S.") Ford, and the owner of the land surrounding Rock Hall Creek. Prior to the arrival of steamboats on the Bay, a fast sailing packet owned by Captain Harris arrived at Bowly's wharf three times each week to transport people, products and mail to the eastern edge of Kent County from Annapolis or Baltimore. Captain Harris was concerned that the steamboats would take his business and did not want them to use Rock Hall Creek as a harbor (even though in previous years it had been the landing point for the daily sailing packet that transferred George Washington and other revolutionaries between North and South). So, the steamboats had to travel an additional twenty-five miles to dock at Grey's Inn Creek (off the Chester River), which more than doubled the steaming time between Baltimore and Rock Hall.

The landing at Grey's Inn Creek was owned by Captain Sharp, and he wanted to control when the steamers would arrive and depart at his property. B. S. Ford was not interested in being told by Captain Sharp or anyone else how to operate his steamboat company. Thus, he acquired some waterfront property at Deep Landing and built a wharf for his steamers. The waterfront property purchased by the Chester River Steamboat Company, with the wharf where the steamer *Gratitude* docked, was near the north end of Lawton Avenue. The property at the end of the road is still a residential estate named "Deep Landing."

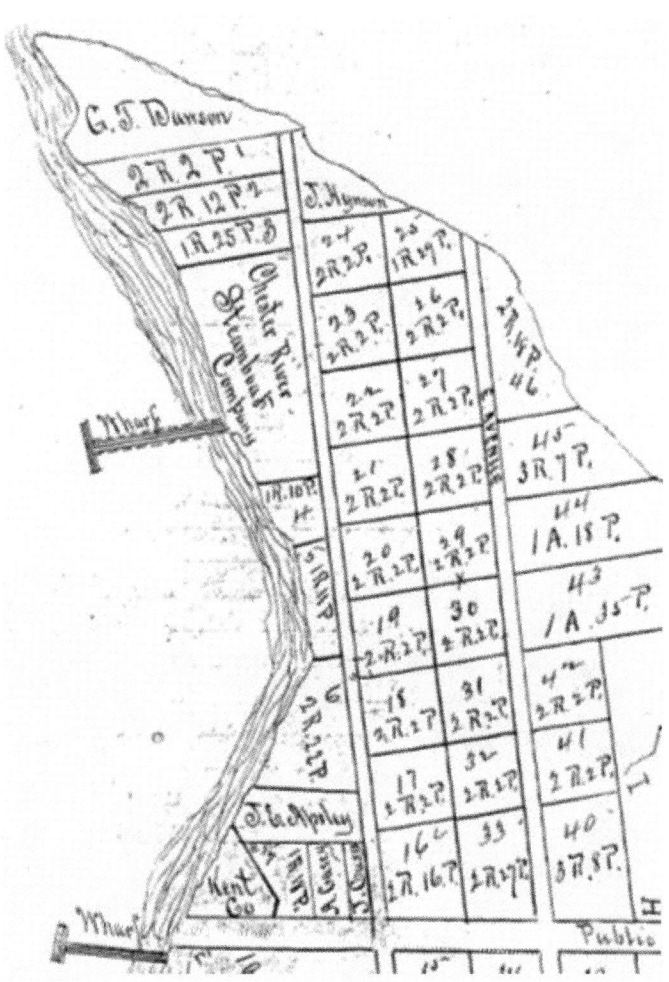

Land Plot from 1890 Showing Proposed Development of the Wilkerson Farm "Deep Landing." A 200-foot wharf to be used by *Gratitude* was built at the property purchased by the Chester River Steamboat Company.

Steamer *Gratitude* at the Wharf in Gratitude

View from *Gratitude* as She Docks at Wharf

Gratitude began arriving at the Deep Landing wharf twice a day in 1887 as she steamed between Baltimore, Rock Hall and Centreville. After some years, people started referring to the wharf and wharf area as "Gratitude" rather than by its historic name, Deep Landing. Even though the steamboat company always referred to the location as Rock Hall in its published schedules, Gratitude became the commonplace name.

For example, a local newspaper in Kent County published the following news item on September 30, 1905:

> "A shark 9-feet long was caught by Capt. Sewell while fishing in the bay. It is at Gratitude Wharf."

In addition to transporting people, *Gratitude* also hauled peaches (in season) and blocks of ice across the Bay. Beginning in the late 1880s, Kent County farmers produced an immense crop of peaches each summer. The steamer would carry a huge load of baskets filled with peaches on each trip back to Baltimore. However, a "yellow blight" destroyed the peach trees in the early 1900s, so the farmers switched to planting tomatoes and, in later years, corn.

On the return trip from Baltimore, *Gratitude* would carry large blocks of ice for delivery to a Rock Hall businessman who made a living selling ice to the seafood industry in Kent County. Ice had become more important after a railroad was built on the Eastern Shore, thereby making it possible to transport fresh seafood directly from Rock Hall to Philadelphia and New York.

On February 9, 1907, an article in the Kent County newspaper described businessmen storing a thousand tons of ice that had been cut from local streams and ponds during a recent severe freeze, but noted that only a third would last until summer – all the rest would melt. Thus, more ice would be needed.

Ice could also hinder the operations of *Gratitude*. The same freezing conditions in February 1907 that resulted in free ice to businesses in Kent County were making it impossible for the steamer to operate. For two weeks the river was so jammed with ice that *Gratitude* could not move; finally, on February 23, 1907, she was able to struggle through the ice as it broke up and reach her wharf.

Gratitude would typically steam along at a modest pace of ten to twelve knots, but even that speed could be considered too fast for conditions. In 1896, the captain of *Gratitude*, William Taylor, was arraigned in court on charges of speeding because he and the masters of other steamers would, on occasion, operate their boats in the Baltimore Harbor channel at speeds that were higher than the legal limits. Although the captains would excuse themselves by saying they were just trying to maintain the schedule and arrive on time, in reality they frequently would be enjoying informal races with each other.

A major change in ownership of *Gratitude* occurred when the Pennsylvania Railroad (PRR), as part of a long-term plan to obtain control of all transportation services on both sides of the Chesapeake Bay, offered in the fall of 1904 to purchase all assets of the Chester River Steamboat Company for the sum of $200,000 (four steamers, wharfs, and properties). The actual offer was made by Henry Scott and Company (a Wilmington banker), who acted as a front man for a new corporation named the Maryland, Delaware and Virginia (MD&V) Railway Company, which was completely owned by the PRR.

The sale was completed on January 3, 1905. No significant changes were made initially, but four months later Captain P. S. McConnor, longtime commander of the steamer *Emma A. Ford*, tendered his resignation and retired. Then, in May 1906, the company changed the name of that steamer from *Emma A. Ford* to *Love Point*.

Although the Chester River Steamboat Company was still a profitable business when it was sold, the transaction occurred at a fortuitous time for the owners. A disastrous fire had started in Baltimore on Sunday morning, February 7, 1904; thirty hours later it had engulfed downtown Baltimore, destroying 1,526 buildings in seventy city blocks, including the steamer piers at Light Street. Many of the steamship companies that were highly dependent on the connection at Baltimore incurred heavy losses during the two years it took the city to rebuild. The financial strength of the PRR enabled the MD&V to withstand the losses resulting from the fire, and *Gratitude* continued operating.

Chester River Steamboat Co.

CHANGE OF SCHEDULE

In Effect Monday, June 6th, 1904

Steamer Gratitude.

Leave Centreville daily except Sunday 7:00 A.M. stopping at the landings on Corsica river, Jackson's Creek and Rock Hall.

Arrive Baltimore about 12 n. Leave Baltimore daily except Sunday 2:30 P.M. for the above named landings. Arrives Centreville about 7:30 P.M.

> GEORGE WARFIELD,
> President.
> J.E. Taylor, General Agent

**Advertisement in a 1904 issue of the
CHESTERTOWN TRANSCRIPT**

This community was shocked Sunday afternoon when it learned that Mr. James Langrall, senior member of the firm of J. Langrall & Bros., who operate canneries at Centreville Landing, had died very suddenly at Winton, the home of Mr. Wm. B. Earle, on the Chester river, about seven miles from Centreville. Accompanied by his wife Mr. Langrall left Baltimore Friday evening with the intention of coming to Centreville, where his canneries were about to begin operation. Mr. Langrall had been complaining for some time of stomach trouble, but appeared to be enjoying his usual health Sunday. He was cheerful at the dinner table and partook of a hearty meal. He arose from the table and shortly after retired to his room. About 4:30 he had occasion to walk across the room, when suddenly he fell across the bed and expired immediately. It is supposed that death was due to heart failure. For several years Mr. Langrall has operated canneries at Centreville Landing, and during that time he has made many friends in this community.

The remains of the deceased were taken to Baltimore Monday afternoon on the steamer *Gratitude* and placed in a vault. Funeral services were held Wednesday afternoon at 2 o'clock, at East Baltimore Station M. E. Church, conducted by Rev. E. L. Hubbard, of Washington, assisted by Revs. W. L. McDowell and W. I. Kenney. Interment was made in Loudon Park, and Masonic services were held at the grave. Delegations from the Royal Areanum, Edin Conclave of Heptasophs, Concordia Lodge of Masons and the Ancient Order of United Workmen attended the funeral.

Steamer *Gratitude* Included in an Obituary

Steamer *Gratitude* at Dock in Baltimore
Steamship Historical Society of America, Inc.
Thomas H. Franklin Collection

***Gratitude* Underway Cruising the Bay**
Rock Hall Museum Collection

The sale also was fortuitous for the captain and crew because they were now employed by a huge, financially strong corporation. On October 1, 1906, the former captain of *Gratitude*, William Taylor, docked his boat at the Light Street pier and walked off. About seventy officers of other steamers joined him in a strike, demanding an immediate raise of fifty percent above their current salaries ($60-$100 per month for captains, $40-$60 for first mates, and $30-$40 for second mates).

The management of MD&V threatened to fire the striking officers and bar them permanently from ever being employed on Bay steamers; the captains retaliated by making public their refusal to move the boats. The strike produced an enormous congestion in Baltimore Harbor, resulting in demands by both business owners and travelers that the owners and captains negotiate. Neither side would.

On October 6, a local newspaper in Kent County became involved on the side of the strikers, and published the following statement:

> "The strike between the masters and pilots and the managers of the steamboat companies is a most unfortunate occurrence. There is no denying the fact there is justice in the demands of the captains and pilots whose duties and responsibilities have been greatly increased, without a corresponding increase in salary. They made a formal demand for more pay which was promptly turned down by the companies. It is certainly hoped that on account of the great loss

to shippers and the inconvenience to all concerned, that the differences will soon be amicably adjusted and the boats placed on their routes."

The strike continued, and one week later the newspaper stated:

> "For two long weeks the tie up between the steamboat companies and the masters and captains has continued with little signs of a settlement. This is surely a most unfortunate mistake on the part of some one, and the investigation made this week by the State authorities places the blame upon the · steamboat companies."

The MD&V concluded on October 12 that it could not win and granted the pay raises. The steamboats were back in business, but the strike did have its consequences. Two weeks after the strike ended, the MD&V permanently abandoned the steamboat schedule on the Baltimore-Earles-Centreville route, part of the Corsica River Line where *Gratitude* had begun its original service on the Eastern Shore of the Bay twenty years previously.

Gratitude continued operating between Rock Hall and Baltimore for another eight years until 1914, when she was sunk in a collision with the steamer *Cambridge* in Eastern Bay (south of Kent Island). The collision with *Cambridge* ended *Gratitude's* service to the people of Rock Hall, and the steamer's history in the years after her departure from Rock Hall was less than glorious.

The year 1914 saw significant changes in two water-related activities in Rock Hall. *Gratitude*, the primary mode of transportation across the Bay, departed, but a new source of entertainment arrived. The *James Adams Floating Theatre* made its first appearance in Rock Hall when it floated into the harbor on Monday, October 26, 1914, and remained there for five days. This novel method of bringing dramatic plays and musicals to the town would last for twenty-seven years (the same length of time that *Gratitude* served Rock Hall). The *James Adams Floating Theatre* was the inspiration and basis for Edna Ferber's famous novel *Show Boat*, which also was produced later as both a movie (two versions) and a highly successful Broadway musical.

Gratitude was raised and repaired after the collision with *Cambridge*, but her owners decided that she was no longer needed because use of steamers to transport passengers and freight around the Chesapeake Bay was declining. Thus, on either October 7 or November 13, 1914, (sources disagree on dates) the MD&V Railroad sold *Gratitude* to the H. E. Bennett North Carolina Line in Norfolk, Virginia. Her new owner advertised her as running excursions (for white people only) from Suffolk to Jamestown.

Steamer *Cambridge* Before the Collision with *Gratitude*

***James Adams Floating Theater* at Dock**

Gratitude's undistinguished service in Virginia received a jolt on December 31, 1917, when she was involved in a collision in Norfolk harbor with an 81-foot yacht, the *Fli-Hawk*. Earlier that year the Navy had free-leased *Fli-Hawk* to serve on patrol duty for the 5th Naval District as part of the local defense efforts during World War I. *Fli-Hawk* sank a few hours after the collision. Three months later, *Gratitude* was acquired by the Navy from Bennett on April 1, 1918, and given registry ID # 3054.

**U.S. Naval Historical Center
Photograph # NH99470**

USS Gratitude (ID # 3054) in port, possibly in the Norfolk, Virginia, area when she was inspected by the Fifth Naval District on June 11, 1918.

Following several months of service in the vicinity of Hampton Roads, Virginia, with a civilian crew, *Gratitude* was given a Navy crew in October 1918 and continued her work supporting Fifth Naval District facilities and Navy ships. During her service in the Navy, she was modified to add an extra deck forward of the pilothouse so that more sailors could be transported during each trip out to a ship at anchor. USS *Gratitude* was returned to her owner on September 15, 1919.

**U.S. Naval Historical Center
Photograph # NH 101352**

USS *Gratitude* (ID # 3054) serving as a supply boat during World War I, with a large number of sailors on board. This photograph was possibly taken from USS *Iowa* (Battleship # 4) in the Hampton Roads area, Virginia, in 1918. A steam launch from Iowa is shown in the foreground.

The final disaster involving *Gratitude* occurred in 1924, when she was severely damaged in a collision with a sunken barge in Norfolk Harbor and later sank. She was carrying 200 passengers, including a group of employees from the Texas Oil Company enjoying an excursion on the Bay, all of whom were rescued.

Gratitude Sinking in Norfolk Harbor
Steamship Historical Society of America, Inc.
Frank O. Braynard Collection

Gratitude was raised and repaired again, but the expenses involved in the accident made her too much of a financial liability. So, on June 30, 1926, *Gratitude* was sold to Mateo Garcia of Havana, Cuba, who renamed her *Cuba*. She then steamed out of American waters and into history.

By the time that *Gratitude* left America, the steamboat industry was in significant decline on the Chesapeake Bay. The arrival of the first automobile in Kent County had occurred on August 8, 1900; a steamboat had transported it from Baltimore to the wharf at Tolchester, a town seven miles north from Rock Hall. After a fifty-minute land trip, the car entered Chestertown. Two decades later, Kent County had numerous paved roads, and trucks were transporting the freight previously conveyed by steamboat.

After *Gratitude* left Rock Hall in 1914, passenger and freight service was provided to the town by the steamer *B. S. Ford* for another nine years. *B. S. Ford* had been the flagship of the Chester River Steamboat Company from 1877 to 1905, and operated for a total of forty-six years on the Chester River and across the Bay to Baltimore. The captain of *B. S. Ford* was William Taylor, former captain of *Gratitude*. The Chester River line ceased operations on December 22, 1923, and the last regularly scheduled steamboat voyage from Rock Hall departed 110 years after the first one had arrived in 1813.

B. S. Ford was sold to a company controlled by the Pennsylvania Railroad, which continued to operate her on a reduced schedule to a variety of towns. After five years of unprofitable operations, *B. S. Ford* was sold on May 21, 1929, to a private individual. The handsome and reliable side-wheeler steamer suffered an ignominious end by having her superstructure, side paddle wheels and engine removed and being used as a lumber barge for thirty years before sinking in the Honga River in Maryland in 1960. A large, hand-built model of *B. S. Ford* is on display in the office of The Sailing Emporium in Rock Hall.

Steamer *B.S. Ford* at the Wharf in Gratitude

A hurricane in August 1933 destroyed at least a third of all remaining wharfs throughout the Bay, and the steamboat companies could not pay to replace them. Since the steamboat industry was already dying from the economic effects of the Great Depression, its inability to recover from the damage caused by the hurricane ensured that the industry would eventually fail. The last steamboat voyage on the Chesapeake Bay occurred in May 1963 aboard the steamer *Bay Belle*, 150 years after the first voyage aboard *Chesapeake*.

And then the steamboats vanished.

Pre-1914 Drawing of Steamer *Gratitude*
(Signed By Lewis E. Perkins, Purser)

Courtesy of Rock Hall Museum

Note what appear to be antlers attached to the structure above the front window of the pilothouse. The photograph of *Gratitude* presented on page 16 of this book shows the same thing. The reason for this somewhat unusual decoration is unknown.

GRATITUDE BEGINS TO CHANGE

During the 1920s, as the era of steamboats faded and the era of cars accelerated, the focus of transportation across the Bay became car ferries. In 1919, the Baltimore and Eastern Shore Ferry Line was created to provide service to Rock Hall from Bay Shore (northeast of Sparrows Point near Baltimore). Car ferries would also serve Tolchester (seven miles north of Rock Hall) and Love Point on Kent Island (seven miles south of Rock Hall).

The first car ferries to serve Rock Hall were purchased in New York and towed to Baltimore for overhaul before beginning service in 1920. They were 190 feet long, 65 feet wide and carried 60 loaded trucks or cars plus passengers. A 250-foot long pier was built from the shoreline in Gratitude out into the bay to accommodate the double-ended ferries (the location of the new pier was about 500 yards south from the wharf where *Gratitude* had docked). The car-ferry pier was built at the end of present-day Route 20 and extended out from the land that now contains Tilghman's Landing condominiums.

The most famous of the car ferries operated by the Baltimore and Eastern Shore Ferry Line during the period from 1931 to 1947 was nicknamed "Smokey Joe." In reality, that name was applied to four successive ferries of the same construction (*Philadelphia, Pittsburgh, Maryland* and *New Brunswick*).

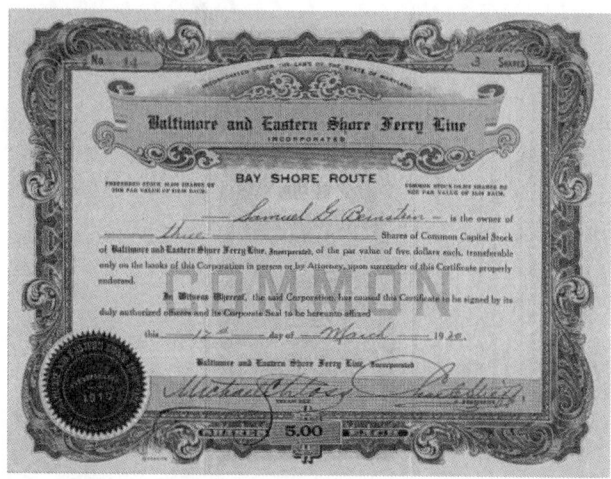

Stock Certificate - Baltimore and Eastern Shore Ferry

Double-Ended Car Ferry at Pier in Gratitude

The last "Smokey Joe" to cross the Bay to Baltimore departed from Love Point (Kent Island) on August 31, 1947; the ferry pier in Gratitude was destroyed by fire a few years later. After the Bay Bridge between Kent Island and Annapolis was completed in 1952, the land area south of where the ferry used to dock in Gratitude was sold off for development; it was named "Ferry Park." Lots there could be purchased then for $250; prices for the same lots in the year 2006 exceeded 1,000 times that amount.

In 1981, despite opposition from nearby property holders, the Town of Rock Hall built a public beach in the Ferry Park area of Gratitude. It is now one of the most popular locations in Rock Hall, especially for viewing spectacular sunsets across the Bay, as the orange-sherbet sun melts into the Chesapeake.

View of Rock Hall From 1943 Postcard
(Looking Southwest toward Annapolis)

The postcard shows Rock Hall Creek (top left) before the large stone jetties were installed to form a protected harbor. Steamboat Wharf Road (now Route 20 - Rock Hall Avenue) is seen at the top right, a long straight road beginning at the western border of Rock Hall and ending at Deep Landing (Gratitude).

The wharf (on Lawton Avenue) where the steamer *Gratitude* docked was off to the top right beyond the edge of the picture. The car ferry pier was on the left side of Route 20 at the end. "Ferry Park" is to the left of the end of Route 20, where nothing but trees can be seen (the entire area is now fully developed).

THE TOWN OF GRATITUDE LIVES ON

Once the passenger steamers and car ferries stopped docking in Gratitude, there was no reason for the people of Rock Hall to go there, and the importance of the area faded quickly. It became a quiet place with a few homes, a small marina on Swan Creek and a restaurant (Fisherman's Wharf) on the water at the end of the road. Two of the old waterfront homes that were viewed by the passengers on *Gratitude* have been restored and are now known as Moonlight Bay Inn and Old Gratitude House.

The original part of the Moonlight Bay Inn and Marina is a Victorian-style house that was built about 1850 and used as the U.S. Post Office for the town of Gratitude beginning in the late 1800s and into the early 1900s. It is situated on property adjacent to the location of the Chester River Steamboat Company wharf used by the steamer *Gratitude* to load passengers and freight traveling between Baltimore on the Western Shore and Rock Hall on the Eastern Shore. After steamboat service ended, the property was used as the Shady Rest Restaurant & Inn, then converted into apartments. New owners purchased the property in 1992; after major rebuilding and renovations, they opened the Moonlight Bay Inn in 1993.

The Old Gratitude House Bed & Breakfast is a Victorian-style house that was originally built about 1890. The front door, entrance hall and dining room fireplace are all that remain of the early home that was once used as a gun club

Moonlight Bay Inn and Marina (Lawton Avenue)

Old Gratitude House B&B (Lawton Avenue)

for hunters in the early 1900s. The house was expanded and became a private family's summer home for many years; those owners named it Old Gratitude House. In 2005, the house was sold, extensively renovated, and converted to a bed and breakfast.

Forty years after the steamer *Gratitude* blasted its whistle in 1914 signaling its final departure from Rock Hall, an exciting announcement appeared in the local newspaper hinting at the possible rebirth of the town. The December 3, 1954, issue of the *Kent County News* said:

> "If War Department approval is forthcoming, Kent will get its second marina, at Swan Point, Gratitude; and Purnell Elbourn, who seeks the permission, is making elaborate plans for its operation. The present restaurant known as Fisherman's Wharf will be an important part of the marina set up."

Painting of Steamer *Gratitude* on Marina Sign

THE FINAL DAYS OF GRATITUDE

The new marina was a success and more people began considering Gratitude as a destination, rather than as a memory. Some new homes were built, old ones were restored, and the future for the town looked promising. But change can have unintended consequences; as the area prospered, the desire for better sewer and water services increased. The solution to obtain them was to become part of Rock Hall.

The town of Gratitude officially disappeared when it was annexed by Rock Hall on February 21, 1977. The "Charter for Rock Hall" was revised to include the following language:

> "...The boundaries of the Town of Rock Hall are hereby extended to include the following area comprised of property lying to the west of the current town boundaries and enclosing an area known as Gratitude and surrounded by the waters of Rock Hall Creek, Chesapeake Bay, Swan Creek and the Haven..."

A large water tower had been erected near the end of Steamboat Wharf Road and the name Gratitude was painted on it. When the water tower was repainted in 2005, the town council decided, after some debate, that the name Rock Hall should be applied rather than Gratitude, much to the dismay of the long-term residents in the Gratitude area.

So, with the stroke of a paintbrush, the town of Gratitude vanished forever, just like the steamboat for which the town had been named.

Newly Painted Water Tower at the End of Maryland Route 20 (Rock Hall Avenue) in Old Gratitude

THE FUTURE: A RETURN TO THE PAST?

Although steamboat service between Rock Hall and Baltimore ended, the desire for water-based transportation between the two sides of the Bay did not. In 1987, the Maryland Department of Transportation (MDOT) completed a feasibility analysis of high-speed (hovercraft-type) waterborne service on four passenger routes from Baltimore to Rock Hall, Annapolis, Kent Island and Cambridge. The report concluded that "...substantial tourist traffic would be required on most of the routes to offset weaker commuter traffic volumes; however, required tourist ridership exceeded the hypothetical capacity of the service..." Thus, no government action resulted.

Private enterprise, however, did take the initiative. In March 1990, *The Washington Post* announced that a new, $1 million, high-speed passenger ferry named *Chesapeake Flyer* would begin operating between Baltimore and Rock Hall. The 50-foot, 105-passenger catamaran (twin-hulled) vessel, which was capable of speeds up to thirty miles per hour, would operate between Baltimore, Annapolis and Rock Hall on Tuesdays through Fridays, then shuttle back and forth between Baltimore and Rock Hall on the weekend. *Chesapeake Flyer* made its first trip on Tuesday, July 24, 1990, but stopped operating after only three days; on the last trip back to Baltimore from Rock Hall that Friday night, the ferry hit an unlighted dredging buoy that was next to the marina where the *Chesapeake Flyer* unloaded it passengers. A compartment in one of the hulls was punctured, and it took until August 16 to repair the damage and resume operations. Ten days later the ferry hit a submerged object in Baltimore's Inner Harbor, damaged a propeller, and slowly made its way back to Rock Hall. Once again, it was taken out of service for repairs. *Chesapeake Flyer* operated for several more years before the company ceased operations in 1994.

Passenger Ferry Similar to *Chesapeake Flyer*
(Bellcraft Industries, Naples, Florida)

Visionaries continued to see the potential for quick transportation across the Bay. In 2004, a company that makes special-use vehicles proposed a revolutionary design that could change all water-based passenger service in the twenty-first century. Maritime Applied Physics Corporation, a ferry designer and builder in Baltimore, has submitted a design to the Coast Guard for certification of an aerodynamic, shallow-draft, all-season ferry that will make the eighteen-mile trip between Rock Hall and Baltimore at forty miles per hour. A new corporation, the Rock Hall Ferry Company, would be established in Rock Hall to operate the service, with multiple round-trips scheduled daily. Service could commence in 2008 if government approval is given and investors are found.

 **Proposed 149-Passenger Design**

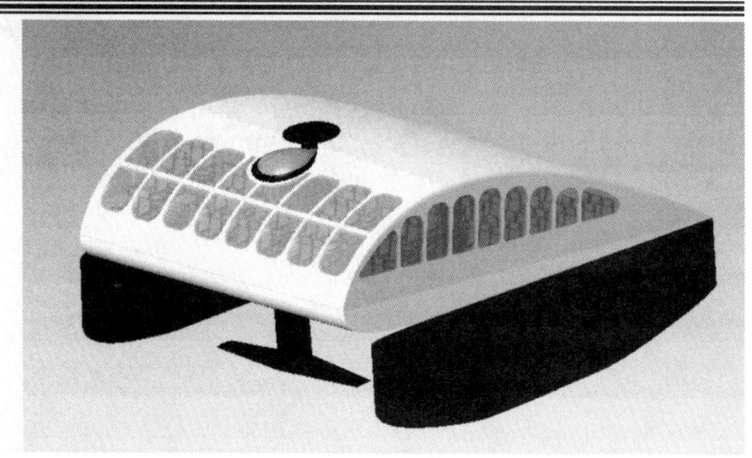

BIBLIOGRAPHY

A Day on the Bay Postcard Views of the Chesapeake, Berth & Anthea Smith, 2001, The Johns Hopkins University Press ISBN 0-8018-6857-2

Charter For Rock Hall, Article II Section 202 C Corporate Limits

Chesapeake Flyer (Newspaper Stories)
> *The Baltimore Daily Record*, February 10, 2006
> *The New York Times*, June 10, 1990
> *The Washington Post*, March 15, 1990; March 17, 1990; April 23, 1990, July 29, 1990; August 1, 1990; August 17, 1990; August 28, 1990; March 18, 1991

Chesapeake Steamboats Vanished Fleet, David C. Holly, 1994, Tidewater Publishers, Centreville, Maryland

Dictionary of American Fighting Ships, www.hazegray.org, Naval Historical Center, Washington, D.C.

From the Early Files, *Kent County News*, Various Editions, 2002 - 2007

General Chronology of the Pennsylvania Railroad Company Predecessors and Successors and Its Historical Context, Christopher T. Baer, February 23, 2007, © Pennsylvania Railroad Technical and Historical Society, Bryn Mawr, PA   www.prrths.com

Gravesend – Serene But Still Profound, Robert J. Johnson, © 1975, Published for the American Revolution Bicentennial Committee of Rock Hall

History of Kent County Maryland 1630-1916, Fred G. Usilton, 1917. Reprinted in 2003 by Janaway Publishing, Santa Maria, California

(Additional 54 Chapters of the) History of Kent County Maryland 1628-1980, William B. Usilton III, 1980, Perry Publications, Chestertown, MD. Kent County Library Index Number MD.975.2 U

Merchant Vessels of the United States, United States Coast Guard Certificate Number 85607, http://www.st.nmfs.gov/st1/CoastGuard/index.html

Online Library of Selected Images, Naval Historical Center, 805 Kidder Breese SE, Washington Navy Yard, Washington, D.C.

Obituary of James Langrall, http://www.rootsweb.com/~mdcbalti/Langrall.html

Stantons' American Steam Vessels The Classic Illustrations Samuel Ward Stanton, 2002, Dover Publications Inc., Mineola, New York. Originally published as American Steam Vessels, 1895, Smith & Stanton

Steamboat on the Chesapeake Emma Giles and the Tolchester Line, David C. Holly, 1987, Tidewater Publishers, Centreville, Maryland

Steamboats on the Chester, Compiled by Dave Blanpied, undated (circa 2000), Printed by the Friends of Eastern Neck

Steamboats Out of Baltimore, Robert H. Burgess and H. Graham Wood, 1968, Tidewater Publishers, Cambridge, Maryland

Steamship Historical Society of America, 1029 Waterman Avenue, East Providence, Rhode Island

Steam Vessels of Chesapeake and Delaware Bays and Rivers American Steam Vessels Series Drawings by Samuel Ward Stanton, Elizabeth S. Anderson, © 1966, Sold by H. Kneeland Whiting, Upper Montclair, New Jersey

Tales of Kent County Volume One, Kevin Hemstock, Editor, ©2006 The Kent County News

The James Adams Floating Theatre, C. Richard Gillespie, 1991, Tidewater Publishers, Centreville, Maryland

Tidewater By Steamboat A Saga of the Chesapeake, David C. Holly, 1991, The Johns Hopkins University Press, Baltimore, Maryland

Twilight on the Bay The Excursion Boat Empire of B.B. Wills, Brian J. Cudahy, 1998, Tidewater Publishers, Centreville, Maryland ISBN 0-87033-509-X (hc)

ABOUT THE AUTHOR

After graduating from Villanova University with a degree in Mechanical Engineering, William M. Denny served for four years as an engineering officer in the U.S. Navy on two destroyers. He then worked for more than thirty years in the commercial nuclear power industry. In January 2006 he retired from engineering to pursue other interests, one of which is history.

The author enjoyed his first steamboat ride in the early 1950s when his parents took him on a ferry to the Statue of Liberty in New York Harbor. In 1999, he fulfilled a dream of many years by cruising on a steamboat, *American Queen*, down the Mississippi River to New Orleans. Three years later, he first learned about the steamboat *Gratitude* and began researching her history.

As the 300th anniversary of the founding of Rock Hall approached (August 11, 2007), the author decided to prepare a brief history about *Gratitude* so that a ship so important to the development of the town would be remembered as part of the celebration. This history was first published in Rock Hall, Maryland, in October 2007.

HELP KEEP HISTORY ALIVE –

SUPPORT THE ROCK HALL MUSEUM!

Two of the illustrations of the steamer *Gratitude* that were used in this book are still in existence only because they were preserved for posterity by the Rock Hall Museum and its dedicated staff of generous volunteers. The museum relies on donations to help ensure that valuable artifacts representing various periods of the town's history are kept safely intact for your enjoyment and the enjoyment of future generations of visitors. For example, in 2007 the museum was given the Audrey Johnson collection of arrowheads and tools used by the native Ozinie tribe who inhabited the Rock Hall area when it was first explored by John Smith in the early 1600s.

Please help the museum volunteers keep history alive by sending a contribution of $20 to the following address:

Rock Hall Museum – *Gratitude*
Town of Rock Hall Municipal Building
5585 Main Street
P.O. Box 367
Rock Hall, Maryland 21661

Thank You!

ORDER FORM FOR ADDITIONAL COPIES

Did you enjoy reading this book and learning about the steamer *Gratitude* and the town named after her? Would you like to order additional copies to give as gifts or use in your book club, library or professional organization?

Cut out (or copy) the order form below, complete the requested information and mail with your check for the full amount. The book(s) will be mailed to you promptly!

Yes, I want to order the book "**DAYS OF *GRATITUDE***"
Mail it to me at the following address:

Name _____

(Please print clearly)

Address _____

_____

Each book costs $9.95 plus $2.05 for shipping & handling, for a total of $12.00 each.

How many books are you ordering? _____
Total amount you have enclosed with this order $_____

Mail this order form and your check to
Biscuit Hill Publications
P.O. Box 14, Rock Hall, MD 21661

Pre-1914 Drawing of Steamer *Gratitude*
(Signed By Lewis E. Perkins, Purser)

Courtesy of Rock Hall Museum